The Four Noble Truths And The Eightfold Path

PAUL CARUS

The Four Noble Truths And The Eightfold Path, P. Carus
Jazzybee Verlag Jürgen Beck
86450 Altenmünster, Loschberg 9
Deutschland

Printed by Createspace, North Charleston, SC, USA

ISBN: 9783849694418

www.jazzybee-verlag.de
www.facebook.com/jazzybeeverlag
admin@jazzybee-verlag.de

CONTENTS:

THUS has it been said by the Buddha, the Enlightened One: It is through not understanding, not realizing four things, that I, Disciples, as well as you, had to wander so long through this round of rebirths. And what are these four things? They are the Noble Truth of Suffering, the Noble Truth of the Origin of Suffering, the Noble Truth of the Extinction of Suffering, the Noble Truth of the Path that leads to the Extinction of Suffering.

As long as the absolutely true knowledge and insight as regards these Four Noble Truths was not quite clear in me, so long was I not sure, whether I had won that supreme Enlightenment which is unsurpassed in all the world with its heavenly beings, evil spirits and gods, amongst all the hosts of ascetics and priests, heavenly beings and men. But as soon as the absolutely true knowledge and insight as regards these Four Noble Truths had become perfectly clear in me, there arose in me the assurance that I had won that supreme Enlightenment unsurpassed.

And I discovered that-profound truth, so difficult to perceive, difficult to understand, tranquilizing and sublime, which is not to be gained by mere reasoning, and is visible only to the wise.

The world, however, is given to pleasure, delighted with pleasure, enchanted with pleasure. Verily, such beings will hardly understand the law of conditionality, the Dependent Origination of every thing; incomprehensible to them will also be the end of all formations, the forsaking of every substratum of rebirth, the fading away of craving; detachment, extinction, Nirvana.

Yet there are beings whose eyes are only a little covered with dust: they will understand the truth.

FIRST TRUTH -
THE NOBLE TRUTH OF SUFFERING

WHAT, now, is the Noble Truth of Suffering?

Birth is suffering; Decay is suffering; Death is suffering; Sorrow, Lamentation, Pain, Grief, and Despair, are suffering; not to get what one desires, is suffering; in short: the Five Groups of Existence are suffering.

What, now, is Birth? The birth of beings belonging to this or that order of beings, their being born, their conception and springing into existence, the manifestation of the groups of existence, the arising of sense activity-this is called Birth.

And what is Decay? The decay of beings belonging to this or that order of beings; their getting aged, frail, grey, and wrinkled; the failing of their vital force, the wearing out of the senses-this is called Decay.

And what is Death? The parting and vanishing of beings out of this or that order of beings, their destruction, disappearance, death, the completion of their life-period, dissolution of the groups of existence, the discarding of the body-this is called Death.

And what is Sorrow? The sorrow arising through this or that loss or misfortune which one encounters, the worrying oneself, the state of being alarmed, inward sorrow, inward woe-this is called Sorrow.

And what is Lamentation? Whatsoever, through this or that loss or misfortune which befalls one, is wail and lament, wailing and lamenting, the state of woe and lamentation this is called Lamentation.

And what is Pain? The bodily pain and unpleasantness, the painful and unpleasant feeling produced by bodily contact-this is called Pain.

And what is Grief? The mental pain and unpleasantness, the painful and unpleasant feeling produced by mental contact-this is called Grief.

And what is Despair? Distress and despair arising through this or that loss or misfortune which one encounters, distressfulness, and desperation-this is called Despair.

And what is the "suffering of not getting what one desires?" To beings subject to birth there comes the desire: "O that we were not subject to birth! O that no new birth was before us!" Subject to decay, disease, death, sorrow, lamentation, pain, grief, and despair, the desire comes to them: "O that we were not subject to these things! O that these things were not before us!" But this cannot be got by mere desiring; and not to get what one desires, is suffering.

THE FIVE GROUPS OF EXISTENCE

And what, in brief, are the Five Groups of Existence? They are Corporeality, Feeling, Perception, [mental] Formations, and Consciousness.

Any corporeal phenomenon, whether one's own or external, gross or subtle, lofty or low, far or near, belongs to the Group of Corporeality; any feeling belongs to the Group of Feeling; any perception belongs to the Group of Perception; any mental formation belongs to the Group of Formations; all consciousness belongs to the Group of Consciousness.

[Our so-called individual existence is in reality nothing but a mere process of these "bodily and mental" phenomena, which since immemorial times was going on before one's apparent birth, and which also after death will continue for immemorial periods of time. In the following, we shall see that these five Groups, or Khandhas-either taken separately, or combined-in no way constitute any real "Ego-entity," and that no Ego-entity exists apart from them, and hence that the belief in an Ego-entity is merely an illusion. Just as that which we designate by the name of "chariot," has no existence apart from axle, wheels, shaft, and so forth: or as the word "house" is merely a convenient designation for various materials put together after a certain fashion so as to enclose a portion of space, and there is no separate house-entity in existence:-in exactly the same way, that which we call a "being," or an "individual," or a "person," or by the name is nothing but a changing combination of physical and psychical phenomena, and has no real existence in itself.]

THE "CORPOREALITY GROUP" OF FOUR ELEMENTS

What, now, is the Group of Corporeality? It is the four primary elements, and Corporeality derived from them.

And what are the four primary elements? They are the Solid Element, the Fluid Element, the Heating Element, the Vibrating Element.

[The four elements, or-to speak more correctly-the four elementary qualities of matter, may be rendered in English as: Inertia, Cohesion, Radiation, and Vibration.

The twenty-four corporeal phenomena which depend upon them are, according to the Abhidharma: eye, ear, nose, tongue, body, visible form, sound, odor, taste, masculinity, femininity, vitality, organ of thinking, gesture, speech, space (cavities of ear, nose, etc.), agility, elasticity, adaptability, growth, duration, decay, variability, change of substance.]

1. What, now, is the Solid Element? The solid element may be one's own, or it may be external. And what is one's own solid element? The

dependent properties, which on one's own person and body are hard and solid, as the hairs of head and body, nails, teeth, skin, flesh, sinews, bones, marrow, kidneys, heart, liver, diaphragm, spleen, lungs, stomach, bowels, mesentery, excrement, or whatever other dependent properties which on one's own person and body are hard and solid-this is called one's own solid element. Now, whether it be one's own solid element, or whether it be the external solid element, they are both only the solid element.

And one should understand, according to reality, and true wisdom: "This does not belong to me; this am I not; this is not my Ego."

2. What, now, is the Fluid Element? The fluid element may be one's own, or it may be external. And what is one own fluid element? The dependent properties, which on one's own person and body are watery or cohesive, as bile, phlegm, pus, blood, sweat, lymph, tears, semen, spit, nasal mucus, oil of the joints, urine or whatever other dependent properties which on one own person and body are watery or cohesive-this is called one's own fluid element. Now, whether it be one's own fluid element, or whether it be the external fluid element, they are both only the fluid element.

And one should understand, according to reality, and true wisdom: "This does not belong to me; this am I not; this is not my Ego."

3. What, now, is the Heating Element? The heating element may be one own, or it may be external. And what is one's own heating element? The dependent properties, which on one's own person and body are heating and radiating, as that whereby one is heated, consumed, scorched, whereby that which has been eaten, drunk, chewed, or tasted, is fully digested; or whatever other dependent properties, which on one's own person and body are heating and radiating this is called one's own heating element. Now, whether it be one's own heating element, or whether it be the external heating element, they are both only the heating element.

And one should understand, according to reality, and true wisdom: "This does not belong to me; this am I not; this is not my Ego."

4. What, now, is the Vibrating Element? The vibrating element may be one's own, or it may be external. And what is one's own vibrating element? The dependent properties, which on one's own person and body are mobile and gaseous, as the upward-going and downward-going winds; the winds of stomach and intestines; in-breathing and out-breathing; or whatever other dependent properties, which on one's own person and body are mobile and gaseous-this is called one's own vibrating element. Now, whether it be one's own vibrating element, or whether it be the external vibrating element, they are both only the vibrating element.

And one should understand, according to reality, and true wisdom: "This does not belong to me; this am I not; this is not my Ego."

Just as one calls "hut" the circumscribed space which comes to be by means of wood and rushes, reeds, and clay, even so we call "body" the circumscribed space that comes to be by means of bones and sinews, flesh and skin.

DEPENDENT ORIGINATION OF CONSCIOUSNESS

Now, though one's eye be intact, yet if the external forms do not fall within the field of vision, and no corresponding conjunction takes place, in that case there occurs no formation of the corresponding aspect of consciousness. Or, though one eye be intact, and the external forms fall within the field of vision, yet if no corresponding conjunction takes place, in that case also there occurs no formation of the corresponding aspect of consciousness. If, however, one's eye is intact, and the external forms fall within the field of vision, and the corresponding conjunction takes place, in that case there arises the corresponding aspect of consciousness.

Hence, I say: the arising of consciousness is dependent upon conditions; and without these conditions, no consciousness arises. And upon whatsoever conditions the arising of consciousness is dependent, after these it is called.

Consciousness whose arising depends on the eye and forms, is called "eye-consciousness."

Consciousness whose arising depends on the ear and sound, is called "ear-consciousness."

Consciousness whose arising depends on the olfactory organ and odors, is called "nose-consciousness."

Consciousness whose arising depends on the tongue and taste, is called "tongue-consciousness."

Consciousness whose arising depends on the body and bodily contacts, is called "body-consciousness."

Consciousness whose arising depends on the mind and ideas, is called "mind-consciousness."

Whatsoever there is of "corporeality" in the consciousness thus arisen, that belongs to the Group of Corporeality. there is of "feeling"-bodily ease, pain, joy, sadness, or indifferent feeling-belongs to the Group of Feeling. Whatsoever there is of "perception"-visual objects, sounds, odors, tastes, bodily impressions, or mind objects-belongs to the Group of Perception. Whatsoever there are of mental "formations" impression, volition, etc.-belong to the Group of mental Formations. Whatsoever there is of "consciousness" therein, belongs to the Group of Consciousness.

And it is impossible that any one can explain the passing out of one existence, and the entering into a new existence, or the growth, increase, and development of consciousness, independent of corporeality, feeling, perception, and mental formations.

THE THREE CHARACTERISTICS OF EXISTENCE

All formations are "transient"; all formations are "subject to suffering"; all things are "without an Ego-entity." Corporeality is transient, feeling is transient, perception is transient, mental formations are transient, consciousness is transient.

And that which is transient, is subject to suffering; and of that which is transient, and subject to suffering and change, one cannot rightly say: "This belongs to me; this am I; this is my Ego."

Therefore, whatever there be of corporeality, of feeling, perception, mental formations, or consciousness, whether one's own or external, whether gross or subtle, lofty or low, far or near, one should understand, according to reality, and true wisdom: "This does not belong to me; this am I not; this is not my Ego."

Suppose, a man who is not blind, were to behold the many bubbles on the Ganges as they are driving along; and he should watch them, and carefully examine them. After carefully examining them, they will appear to him empty, unreal, and unsubstantial. In exactly the same way, does the monk behold all the corporeal phenomena, feelings, perceptions, mental formations, and states of consciousness-whether they be of the past, or the present, or the future, far, or near. And he watches them, and examines them carefully; and, after carefully examining them, they appear to him empty, void, and without an Ego

Whoso delights in corporeality, or feeling, or perception, or mental formations, or consciousness, he delights in suffering; and whoso delights in suffering, will not be freed from suffering. Thus I say

How can you find delight and mirth,
Where there is burning without end?
In deepest darkness you are wrapped!
Why do you not seek for the light?
Look at this puppet here, well rigged,
A heap of many sores, piled up,
Diseased, and full of greediness,
Unstable, and impermanent!
Devoured by old age is this frame,
A prey of sickness, weak and frail;
To pieces breaks this putrid body,
All life must truly end in death.

THE THREE WARNINGS

Did you never see in the world a man, or a woman, eighty, ninety, or a hundred years old, frail, crooked as a gable roof, bent down, resting on crutches, with tottering steps, infirm, youth long since fled, with broken teeth, grey and scanty hair, or bald-headed, wrinkled, with blotched limbs? And did the thought never come to you that also you are subject to decay, that also you cannot escape it?

Did you never see in the world a man, or a woman, who being sick, afflicted, and grievously ill, and wallowing in his own filth, was lifted up by some people, and put to bed by others? And did the thought never come to you that also you are subject to disease, that also you cannot escape it?

Did you never see in the world the corpse of a man, or a woman, one, or two, or three days after death, swollen up, blue-black in color, and full of corruption? And did the thought never come to you that also you are subject to death, that also you cannot escape it?

SAMSARA, THE WHEEL OF EXISTENCE

Inconceivable is the beginning of this Samsara; not to be discovered is any first beginning of beings, who, obstructed by ignorance, and ensnared by craving, are hurrying and hastening through this round of rebirths.

[Samsara-the Wheel of Existence, lit., the "Perpetual Wandering"-is the name by which is designated the sea of life ever restlessly heaving up and down, the symbol of this continuous process of ever again and again being born, growing old, suffering, and dying. More precisely Put: Samsara is the unbroken chain of the fivefold Khandha-combinations, which, constantly changing from moment to moment, follow continuously one upon the other through inconceivable periods of time. Of this Samsara, a single lifetime constitutes only a vanishingly tiny fraction; hence, to be able to comprehend the first noble truth, one must let one's gaze rest upon the Samsara, upon this frightful chain of rebirths, and not merely upon one single lifetime, which, of course, may be sometimes not very painful.]

Which do you think is the more: the flood of tears, which weeping and wailing you have shed upon this long way-hurrying and hastening through this round of rebirths, united with the undesired, separated from the desired this, or the waters of the four oceans?

Long time have you suffered the death of father and mother, of sons, daughters, brothers, and sisters. And whilst you were thus suffering, you have, verily, shed more tears upon this long way than there is water in the four oceans.

Which do you think is the more: the streams of blood that, through your being beheaded, have flowed upon this long way, or the waters in the four oceans?

Long time have you been caught as dacoits, or highwaymen, or adulterers; and, through your being beheaded, verily, more blood has flowed upon this long way than there is water in the four oceans.

But how is this possible?

Inconceivable is the beginning of this Samsara; not to be discovered is any first beginning of beings, who, obstructed by ignorance, and ensnared by craving, are hurrying and hastening through this round of rebirths.

And thus have you long time undergone suffering, undergone torment, undergone misfortune, and filled the graveyards full; verily, long enough to be dissatisfied with all the forms of existence, long enough to turn away, and free yourselves from them all.

SECOND TRUTH - THE NOBLE TRUTH OF THE ORIGIN OF SUFFERING

WHAT, now, is the Noble Truth of the Origin of Suffering? It is that craving which gives rise to fresh rebirth, and, bound up with pleasure and lust, now here, now there, finds ever fresh delight.

[In the absolute sense, it is no real being, no self-determined, unchangeable, Ego-entity that is reborn. Moreover, there is nothing that remains the same even for two consecutive moments; for the Five Khandhas, or Groups of Existence, are in a state of perpetual change, of continual dissolution and renewal. They die every moment, and every moment new ones are born. Hence it follows that there is no such thing as a real existence, or "being" (Latin esse), but only as it were an endless process, a continuous change, a "becoming," consisting in a "producing," and in a "being produced"; in a "process of action," and in a "process of reaction," or "rebirth."

This process of perpetual "producing" and "being produced" may best be compared with an ocean wave. In the case of a wave, there is not the slightest quantity of water traveling over the surface of the sea. But the wave structure, that hastens over the surface of the water, creating the appearance of one and the same mass of water, is, in reality, nothing but the continuous rising and falling of continuous, but quite different, masses of water, produced by the transmission of force generated by the wind. Even so, the Buddha did not teach that Ego-entities hasten through the ocean of rebirth, but merely life-waves, which, according to their nature and activities (good, or evil), manifest themselves here as men, there as animals, and elsewhere as invisible beings.]

THE THREEFOLD CRAVING

There is the "Sensual Craving," the "Craving for Eternal-Annihilation." Existence," the "Craving for Self-Annihilation."

[The "Craving for Eternal Existence," according to the Visuddhi-Magga, is intimately connected with the so-called Eternity-Belief," i.e., the belief in an absolute, eternal, Ego-entity persisting independently of our body.

The Craving for Self-Annihilation is the outcome of the so-called "Annihilation-Belief," the delusive materialistic notion of an Ego which is annihilated at death, and which does not stand in any causal relation with the time before birth or after death.]

But, where does this craving arise and take root? Wherever in the world there are delightful and pleasurable things, there this craving arises and takes root. Eye, ear, nose, tongue, body, and mind, are delightful and pleasurable: there this craving arises and takes root.

Visual objects, sounds, smells, tastes, bodily impressions, and mind-objects, are delightful and pleasurable: there this craving arises and takes root.

Consciousness, sense impression, feeling born of sense impression, perception, will, craving, thinking, and reflecting, are delightful and pleasurable: there this craving arises and takes root.

If, namely, when perceiving a visual object, a sound, odor, taste, bodily impression, or a mind object, the object is pleasant, one is attracted; and if unpleasant, one is repelled.

Thus, whatever kind of "Feeling" one experiences, pleasant, unpleasant, or indifferent-one approves of, and cherishes the feeling, and clings to it; and while doing so, lust springs up; but lust for feelings, means Clinging; and on Clinging, depends the "Process of Becoming"; on the Process of Becoming (Karma-process), depends (future) "Birth"; and dependent on Birth, are Decay and Death, Sorrow, Lamentation, Pain, Grief, and Despair. Thus arises this whole mass of suffering.

This is called the Noble Truth of the Origin of Suffering.

HEAPING UP OF PRESENT SUFFERING

Verily, due to sensuous craving, conditioned through sensuous craving, impelled by sensuous craving, entirely moved by sensuous craving, kings fight with kings, princes with princes, priests with priests, citizens with citizens; the mother quarrels with the son, the son with the mother, the father with the son, the son with the father; brother quarrels with brother, brother with sister, sister with brother, friend with friend. Thus, given to dissension, quarreling and fighting, they fall upon one another with fists, sticks, or weapons. And thereby they suffer death or deadly pain.

And further, due to sensuous craving, conditioned through sensuous craving, impelled by sensuous craving, entirely moved by sensuous craving, people break into houses, rob, plunder, pillage whole houses, commit highway robbery, seduce the wives of others. Then, the rulers have such people caught, and inflict on them various forms of punishment. And thereby they incur death or deadly pain. Now, this is the misery of sensuous craving, the heaping up of suffering in this present life, due to sensuous craving, conditioned through sensuous craving, caused by sensuous craving, entirely dependent on sensuous craving.

HEAPING UP OF FUTURE SUFFERING

And further, people take the evil way in deeds, the evil way in words, the evil way in thoughts; and by taking the evil way in deeds, words, and thoughts, at the dissolution of the body, after death, they fall into a downward state of existence, a state of suffering, into perdition, and the abyss of hell. But, this is the misery of sensuous craving, the heaping up of suffering in the future life, due to sensuous craving, conditioned through sensuous craving, caused by sensuous craving, entirely dependent on sensuous craving.

Not in the air, nor ocean-midst,
Nor hidden in the mountain clefts,
Nowhere is found a place on earth,
Where man is freed from evil deeds.

INHERITANCE OF DEEDS (KARMA)

For, owners of their deeds (karma) are the beings, heirs of their deeds; their deeds are the womb from which they sprang; with their deeds they are bound up; their deeds are their refuge. Whatever deeds they do-good or evil-of such they will be the heirs.

And wherever the beings spring into existence, there their deeds will ripen; and wherever their deeds ripen, there they will earn the fruits of those deeds, be it in this life, or be it in the next life, or be it in any other future life.

There will come a time, when the mighty ocean will dry up, vanish, and be no more. There will come a time, when the mighty earth will be devoured by fire, perish, and be no more. But, yet there will be no end to the suffering of beings, who, obstructed by ignorance, and ensnared by craving, are hurrying and hastening through this round of rebirths.

THIRD TRUTH - THE NOBLE TRUTH OF THE EXTINCTION OF SUFFERING

WHAT, now, is the Noble Truth of the Extinction of Suffering? It is the complete fading away and extinction of this craving, its forsaking and giving up, the liberation and detachment from it.

But where may this craving vanish, where may it be extinguished? Wherever in the world there are delightful and pleasurable things, there this craving may vanish, there it may be extinguished.

Be it in the past, present, or future, whosoever of the monks or priests regards the delightful and pleasurable things in the world as "impermanent," "miserable," and "without an Ego," as a disease and cancer; it is he who overcomes the craving.

And released from Sensual Craving, released from the Craving for Existence, he does not return, does not enter again into existence.

DEPENDENT EXTINCTION OF ALL PHENOMENA

For, through the total fading away and extinction of Craving, Clinging is extinguished; through the extinction of clinging, the Process of Becoming is extinguished; through the extinction of the (karmic) process of becoming, Rebirth is extinguished; and through the extinction of rebirth, Decay and Death, Sorrow, Lamentation, Suffering, Grief, and Despair, are extinguished. Thus comes about the extinction of this whole mass of suffering.

Hence, the annihilation, cessation, and overcoming of corporeality, feeling, perception, mental formations, and consciousness, this is the extinction of suffering, the end of disease, the overcoming of old age and death.

[The undulatory motion, which we call wave-which in the spectator creates the illusion of a single mass of water moving over the surface of the lake-is produced and fed by the wind, and maintained by the stored-up energies. After the wind has ceased, and no fresh wind again whips up the water, the stored-up energies will gradually be consumed, and the whole undulatory motion come to an end. Similarly, if fire does not get new fuel, it will become extinct. just so, this Five-Khandha-process-which, in the ignorant worldling, creates the illusion of an Ego-entity-is produced and fed by the life-affirming craving, and maintained for some time by means of the stored-up life-energies. Now, after the fuel, i.e., the craving and clinging to life, has ceased, and no new craving impels again this Five-Khandha-process, life will continue as long as there are still life-energies stored up, but at their destruction at death, the Five-Khandha-process will reach final extinction.

Thus, nirvana or "Extinction" (Sanskrit: to cease blowing, to become extinct), may be considered under two aspects:

1. "Extinction of Impurities," reached at the attainment of Arahatship, or Holiness, which takes place during the life-time.

2. "Extinction of the Five-Khandha-process," which takes place at the death of the Arahat.]

NIRVANA

This, truly, is the Peace, this is the Highest, namely the end of all formations, the forsaking of every substratum of rebirth, the fading away of craving: detachment, extinction-Nirvana.

Enraptured with lust, enraged with anger, blinded by delusion, overwhelmed, with mind ensnared, man aims at his own ruin, at others' ruin, at the ruin of both parties, and he experiences mental pain and grief. But, if lust, anger, and delusion are given up, man aims neither at his own ruin, nor at others' ruin, nor at the ruin of both parties, and he experiences no mental pain and grief. Thus is Nirvana immediate, visible in this life, inviting, attractive, and comprehensible to the wise.

The extinction of greed, the extinction of anger, the extinction of delusion: this, indeed, is called Nirvana.

THE ARAHAT, OR HOLY ONE

And for a disciple thus freed, in whose heart dwells peace, there is nothing to be added to what has been done, and naught more remains for him to do. Just as a rock of one solid mass remains unshaken by the wind, even so, neither forms, nor sounds, nor odors, nor tastes, nor contacts of any kind, neither the desired, nor the undesired, can cause such an one to waver. Steadfast is his mind, gained is deliverance.

And he who has considered all the contrasts on this earth, and is no more disturbed by anything whatever in the world, the Peaceful One, freed from rage, from sorrow, and from longing, he has passed beyond birth and decay.

THE IMMUTABLE

There is a realm, where there is neither the solid, nor the fluid, neither heat, nor motion, neither this world, nor any other world, neither sun, nor moon. This I call neither arising, nor passing away, neither standing still nor being born, nor dying. There is neither foothold, nor development, nor any basis. This is the end of suffering.

There is an Unborn, Unoriginated, Uncreated, Unformed. If there were not this Unborn, this Unoriginated, this Uncreated, this Unformed, escape from the world of the born, the originated, the created, the formed, would not be possible.

But since there is an Unborn, Unoriginated, Uncreated, Unformed, therefore is escape possible from the world of the born, the originated, the created, the formed.

FOURTH TRUTH - THE NOBLE TRUTH OF THE PATH THAT LEADS TO THE EXTINCTION OF SUFFERING THE TWO EXTREMES AND THE MIDDLE PATH

TO GIVE oneself up to indulgence in sensual pleasure, the base, common, vulgar, unholy, unprofitable; and also to give oneself up to self-mortification, the painful, unholy, unprofitable: both these two extremes the Perfect One has avoided, and found out the Middle Path, which makes one both to see and to know, which leads to peace, to discernment, to enlightenment, to Nirvana.

THE EIGHTFOLD PATH

It is the Noble Eightfold Path, the way that leads to the extinction of suffering, namely:

1. Right Understanding,
2. Right Mindedness, which together are Wisdom.
3. Right Speech,
4. Right Action,
5. Right Living, which together are Morality.
6. Right Effort,
7. Right Attentiveness,
8. Right Concentration, which together are Concentration.

This is the Middle Path which the Perfect One has found out, which makes one both to see and to know, which leads to peace, to discernment, to enlightenment, to Nirvana.

Free from pain and torture is this path, free from groaning and suffering; it is the perfect path.

Truly, like this path there is no other path to the purity of insight. If you follow this path, you will put an end to suffering.

But each one has to struggle for himself, the Perfect Ones have only pointed out the way.

Give ear then, for the Immortal is found. I reveal, I set forth the Truth. As I reveal it to you, so act! And that supreme goal of the holy life, for the sake of which, sons of good families rightly go forth from home to the homeless state: this you will, in no long time, in this very life, make known to yourself, realize, and make your own.

FIRST STEP - RIGHT UNDERSTANDING

WHAT, now, is Right Understanding? It is understanding the Four Truths. To understand suffering; to understand the origin of suffering; to understand the extinction of suffering; to understand the path that leads to the extinction of suffering: This is called Right Understanding

Or, when the noble disciple understands what is karmically wholesome, and the root of wholesome karma; what is karmically unwholesome, and the root of unwholesome karma, then he has Right Understanding.

["Karmically unwholesome" is every volitional act of body, speech, or mind which is rooted in greed, hatred, or delusion, and produces evil and painful results in this or any future form of existence.]

What, now, is "karmically unwholesome?"

In Bodily Action it is destruction of living beings; stealing; and unlawful sexual intercourse. In Verbal Action it is lying; tale-bearing; harsh language; and frivolous talk. In Mental Action it is covetousness; ill-will; and wrong views.

And what is the root of unwholesome karma? Greed is a root of unwholesome karma; Anger is a root of unwholesome karma; Delusion is a root of unwholesome karma.

[The state of greed, as well as that of anger, is always accompanied by delusion; and delusion, ignorance, is the primary root of all evil.]

Therefore, I say, these demeritorious actions are of three kinds: either due to greed, or due to anger, or due to delusion.

What, now, is "karmically wholesome?"

In Bodily Action it is to abstain from killing; to abstain from stealing; and to abstain from unlawful sexual intercourse.

In Verbal Action it is to abstain from lying; to abstain from tale-bearing; to abstain from harsh language; and to abstain from frivolous talk.

In Mental Action it is absence of covetousness; absence of ill-will; and right understanding.

And what is the root of wholesome karma? Absence of greed (unselfishness) is a root of wholesome karma; absence of anger (benevolence) is a root of wholesome karma; absence of delusion (wisdom) is a root of wholesome karma.

Or, when one understands that corporeality, feeling, perception, mental formation, and consciousness, are transient [subject to suffering, and without an Ego], also in that case one possesses Right Understanding.

UNPROFITABLE QUESTIONS

Should anyone say that he does not wish to lead the holy life under the Blessed One, unless the Blessed One first tells him, whether the world is eternal or temporal, finite or infinite; whether the life principle is identical with the body, or something different; whether the Perfect One continues after death, and so on such a man would die, ere the Perfect One could tell him all this.

It is as if a man were pierced by a poisoned arrow, and his friends, companions, or near relations, should send for a surgeon; but that man should say: "I will not have this arrow pulled out, until I know who the man is that has wounded me: whether he is a noble, a priest, a citizen, or a servant"; or: "what his name is, and to what family he belongs"; or: "whether he is tall, or short, or of medium height." Verily, such a man would die, ere he could adequately learn all this.

Therefore, the man who seeks his own welfare, should pull out this arrow-this arrow of lamentation, pain, and sorrow.

For, whether the theory exists, or whether it does not exist, that the world is eternal, or temporal, or finite, or infinite-certainly, there is birth, there is decay, there is death, sorrow, lamentation, pain, grief, and despair, the extinction of which, attainable even in this present life, I make known unto you.

There is, for instance, an unlearned worldling, void of regard for holy men, ignorant of the teaching of holy men, untrained in the noble doctrine. And his heart is possessed and overcome by Self-Illusion, by Skepticism, by attachment to mere Rule and Ritual, by Sensual Lust, and by will; and how to free himself from these things, he does not really know.

[Self-Illusion may reveal itself as "Eternalism" or Eternity-belief" i.e., the belief that one's Ego is existing independently of the material body, and continuing even after the dissolution of the latter; or as "Annihilationism," or "Annihilation-belief" i.e., the materialistic belief that this present life constitutes the Ego, and hence that it is annihilated at the death of the material body.]

Not knowing what is worthy of consideration, and what is unworthy of consideration, he considers the unworthy, and not the worthy.

And unwisely he considers thus: "Have I been in the past? Or. have I not been in the past? What have I been in the past? How have I been in the past? From what state into what state did I change in the past?-Shall I be in the future? Or, shall I not be in the future? What shall I be in the future? How shall I be in the future? From what state into what state shall I change in the future?" And the present also fills him with doubt: "Am I? Or, am I not? What am I? How am I? This being, whence has it come? Whither will it go?"

And with such unwise considerations, he falls into one or other of the six views, and it becomes his conviction and firm belief: "I have an Ego"; or: "I have no Ego"; or: "With the Ego I perceive the Ego"; or: "With that which is no Ego, I perceive the Ego"; or: "With the Ego I perceive that which is no Ego. Or, he falls into the following view: "This my Ego, which can think and feel, and which, now here, now there, experiences the fruit of good and evil deeds; this my Ego is permanent, stable, eternal, not subject to change, and will thus eternally remain the same."

If there really existed the Ego, there would be also something which belonged to the Ego. As, however, in truth and reality, neither the Ego, nor anything belonging to the Ego, can be found, is it not therefore really an utter fool's doctrine to say: "This is the world, this am I; after death, I shall be permanent, persisting, and eternal?"

These are called mere views, a thicket of views, a puppet show of views, a toil of views, a snare of views; and ensnared in the fetter of views, the ignorant worldling will not be freed from rebirth, from decay, and from death, from sorrow, pain, grief, and despair; he will not be freed, I say, from suffering.

THE SOTAPAN, OR "STREAM-ENTERER"

The learned and noble disciple, however, who has regard for holy men, knows the teaching of holy men, is well trained in the noble doctrine, he understands what is worthy of consideration, and what is unworthy. And knowing this, he considers the worthy, and not the unworthy. What suffering is, he wisely considers. What the origin of suffering is, he wisely considers; what the extinction of suffering is, he wisely considers; what the path is that leads to the extinction of suffering, he wisely considers.

And by thus considering, three fetters vanish, namely: Self-illusion, Skepticism, and Attachment to mere Rule and Ritual.

But those disciples in whom these three fetters have vanished have "entered the Stream," have forever escaped the states of woe, and are assured of final enlightenment.

> More than any earthly power,
> More than all the joys of heaven,
> More than rule o'er all the world,
> Is the Entrance to the Stream.

And, verily, those who are filled with unshaken faith in me, all those have entered the stream.

There are ten "Fetters" by which beings are bound to the wheel of existence. They are: Self-Illusion, Skepticism, Attachment to mere Rule and

Ritual, Sensual Lust, Ill-will, Craving for the World of pure Form, Craving for the Formless World, Conceit, Restlessness, Ignorance.

A Sotapan, or "Stream-Enterer" i.e. "one who has entered the stream leading to Nirvana," is free from the first three fetters.

A Sakadagamin, or "Once-Returned"-namely to this sensuous sphere-has overcome the 4th and 5th fetters in their grosser form. An Anagamin, or "Non-Returner," is wholly freed from the first five fetters, which bind to rebirth in the sensuous sphere; after death, whilst living in the sphere of pure form, he will reach the goal. An Arahat, or perfectly "Holy One," is freed from all fetters.]

THE TWO UNDERSTANDINGS

Therefore, I say, Right Understanding is of two kinds:

1. The view that alms and offerings are not useless; that there is fruit and result, both of good and bad actions; that there are such things as this life, and the next life; that father and mother as spontaneously born beings (in the heavenly worlds) are no mere words; that there are monks and priests who are spotless and perfect, who can explain this life and the next life, which they themselves have understood: this is called the "Mundane Right Understanding," which yields worldly fruits, and brings good results.

2. But whatsoever there is of wisdom, of penetration, of right understanding, conjoined with the Path-the mind being turned away from the world, and conjoined with the path, the holy path being turned away from the world, and conjoined with the path, the holy path being pursued;-this is called the "Ultramundane Right Understanding," which is not of the world, but is ultramundane, and conjoined with the Path.

[Thus, there are two kinds of the Eightfold Path: the "mundane," practiced by the "worldling"; and the "ultra-mundane," practiced by the "Noble Ones."]

Now, in understanding wrong understanding as wrong, and right understanding as right, one practices Right Understanding [1st step]; and in making efforts to overcome wrong understanding, and to arouse right understanding, one practices. Right Effort [6th step]; and in overcoming wrong understanding with attentive mind, and dwelling with attentive mind in the possession of right understanding, one practices Right-Attentiveness [7th step]. Hence, there are three things that accompany and follow upon right understanding, namely: right understanding, right effort, and right attentiveness.

Now, if any one should put the question, whether I admit any view at all, he should be answered thus:

The Perfect One is free from any theory, for the Perfect One has understood what corporeality is, and how it arises, and passes away. He has understood what feeling is, and how it arises, and passes away. He has understood what perception is, and how it arises, and passes away. He has understood what the mental formations are, and how they arise, and pass away. He has understood what consciousness is, and how it arises, and passes away. Therefore, I say, the Perfect One has won complete deliverance through the extinction, fading-away, disappearance, rejection, and getting rid of all opinions and conjectures, of all inclination to the vainglory of "I" and "mine."

Whether Perfect Ones [Buddhas] appear in the world or whether Perfect Ones do not appear in the world, it still remains a firm condition, an immutable fact and fixed law: that all formations are impermanent" that all formations are "subject to suffering"; that everything is "without an Ego."

[The word sankhara (formations) comprises all things which have a beginning and an end, the so-called created, or "formed" things, i.e., all possible physical and mental constituents of existence.]

A corporeal phenomenon, a feeling, a perception, a mental formation, a consciousness, that is permanent and persistent, eternal and not subject to change: such a thing the wise men in this world do not recognize; and I also say, there is no such thing.

And it is impossible that a being possessed of Right Understanding should regard anything as the Ego.

Now, if someone should say that Feeling is his Ego, he should be answered thus: "There are three kinds of feeling: pleasurable, painful, and indifferent feeling. Which of these three feelings, now, do you consider your Ego?" At the moment namely of experiencing one of these feelings one does not experience the other two. These three kinds of feelings are impermanent, of dependent origin, are subject to decay and dissolution, to fading-away and extinction. Whosoever, in experiencing one of these feelings, thinks that this is his Ego, will, after the extinction of that feeling, admit that his Ego has become dissolved. And thus he will consider his Ego already in this present life as impermanent, mixed up with pleasure and pain, subject to rising and passing away.

If any one should say that Feeling is not his Ego, and that his Ego is inaccessible to feeling, he should be asked thus: "Now, where there is no feeling, is it there possible to say: 'This am I?'"

Or, someone might say: "Feeling, indeed, is not my Ego, but it also is untrue that my Ego is inaccessible to feeling; for it is my Ego that feels, for my Ego has the faculty of feeling." Such a one should be answered thus: "Suppose, feeling should become altogether totally extinguished; now, if there, after the extinction of feeling, no feeling whatever exists, it is then possible to say: 'This am I?'"

To say that the mind, or the mind-objects, or the mind-consciousness, constitute the Ego; such an assertion is unfounded. For an arising and a passing away is seen there; and seeing this, one should come to the conclusion that one's Ego arises and passes away.

It would be better for the unlearned worldling to regard this body, built up of the four elements, as his Ego, rather than the mind. For it is evident that this body may last for a year, for two years, for three years, four, five, or ten years, or even a hundred years and more; but that which is called thought, or mind, or consciousness, is continuously, during day and night, arising as one thing, and passing away as another thing.

Therefore, whatsoever there is of corporeality, of feeling, of perception, of mental formations, of consciousness, whether one's own or external, gross or subtle, lofty or low, far or near; there one should understand according to reality and true wisdom: "This does not belong to me; this am I not; this is not my Ego."

[To show the Egolessness, utter emptiness of existence, Visuddhi-Magga XVI quotes the following verse:

Mere suffering exists, no sufferer is found;
The deed is, but no doer of the deed is there;
Nirvana is, but not the man that enters it;
The Path is, but no traveler on it is seen.]

PAST, PRESENT, AND FUTURE

If, now, any one should ask: "Have you been in the past, and is it untrue that you have not been? Will you be in the future, and is it untrue that you will not be? Are you, and is it untrue that you are not?"-you may say that you have been in the past, and it is untrue that you have not been; that you will be in the future, and it is untrue that you will not be; that you are, and it is untrue that you are not.

In the past only the past existence was real, but unreal the future and present existence. In the future only the future existence will be real, but unreal the past and present existence. Now only the present existence is real, but unreal the past and future existence.

Verily, he who perceives the Dependent Origination, perceives the truth and he who perceives the truth, perceives the dependent origination. For, just as from the cow comes milk, from milk curds, from curds butter, from butter ghee, from ghee the scum of ghee; and when it is milk, it is not counted as curds, or butter, or ghee, or scum of ghee, but only as milk; and when it is curds, it is only counted as curds-just so was my past existence at that time real, but unreal the future and present existence; and my future existence will be at one time real, but unreal the past and present existence; and my present existence is now real, but unreal the past and future existence. All these are merely popular designations and expressions, mere conventional terms of speaking, mere popular notions. The Perfect One, indeed, makes use of these, without, however, clinging to them.

Thus, he who does not understand corporeality, feeling, perception, mental formations and consciousness according to reality [i.e., as void of a personality, or Ego], and not their arising, their extinction, and the way to their extinction, he is liable to believe, either that the Perfect One continues after death, or that he does not continue after death, and so forth.

Verily, if one holds the view that the vital principle [Ego] is identical with this body, in that case a holy life is not possible; or, if one holds the view that the vital principle is something quite different from the body, in that case also a holy life is not possible. Both these two Extremes the Perfect One has avoided, and shown the Middle Doctrine, saying:

DEPENDENT ORIGINATION

On Delusion depend the Karma-Formations. On the karma-formations depends Consciousness [starting with rebirth-consciousness in the womb of the mother].- On consciousness depends the Mental and Physical Existence.-On the mental and physical existence depend the Six Sense-Organs.-On the six sense-organs depends the Sensory Impression.-On the sensory impression depends Feeling.-On feeling depends; Craving.-On craving depends Clinging. On clinging depends the Process of Becoming.-On the process of becoming [here: karmaprocess] depends Rebirth.-On rebirth depend Decay and Death, sorrow, lamentation, pain, grief and despair. Thus arises this whole mass of suffering. This is called the noble truth of the origin of suffering.

In whom, however, Delusion has disappeared and wisdom arisen, such a disciple heaps up neither meritorious, nor demeritorious, nor imperturbable Karma-formations.

Thus, through the entire fading away and extinction of this Delusion, the Karma-Formations are extinguished. Through the extinction of the Karma-formations, Consciousness [rebirth] is extinguished. Through the extinction of consciousness, the Mental and Physical Existence is extinguished. Through the extinction of the mental and physical existence, the six Sense-Organs are extinguished. Through the extinction of the six sense-organs, the Sensory Impression is extinguished. Through the extinction of the sensory impression, Feeling is extinguished. Through the extinction of feeling, Craving is extinguished. Through the extinction of craving, Clinging is extinguished. Through the extinction of clinging, the Process of Becoming is extinguished. Through the extinction of the process of becoming, Rebirth is extinguished. Through the extinction of rebirth, Decay and Death, sorrow, lamentation, pain, grief and despair are extinguished. Thus takes place the extinction of this whole mass of suffering. This is called the Noble Truth of the Extinction of Suffering.

KARMA: REBIRTH - PRODUCING AND BARREN

Verily, because beings, obstructed by Delusion, and ensnared by Craving, now here now there seek ever fresh delight, therefore such action comes to ever fresh Rebirth.

And the action that is done out of greed, anger and delusion, that springs from them, has its source and origin there: this action ripens wherever one is reborn; and wherever this action ripens, there one experiences the fruits of this action, be it in this life, or the next life, or in some future life.

However, through the fading away of delusion through the arising of wisdom, through the extinction of craving, no future rebirth takes place again

For the actions, which are not done out of greed, anger and delusion, which have not sprung from them, which have not their source and origin there-such actions are, through the absence of greed, anger and delusion, abandoned, rooted out, like a palm-tree torn out of the soil, destroyed, and not liable to spring up again.

In this respect one may rightly say of me: that I teach annihilation, that I propound my doctrine for the purpose of annihilation, and that I herein train my disciples; for, certainly, I do teach annihilation-the annihilation, namely, of greed, anger and delusion, as well as of the manifold evil and unwholesome things.

["Dependent Origination" is the teaching of the strict conformity to law of everything that happens, whether in the realm of the physical, or the psychical. It shows how the totality of phenomena, physical and mental, the entire phenomenal world that depends wholly upon the six senses, together with all its suffering-and this is the vital point of the teaching is not the mere play of blind chance, but has an existence that is dependent upon conditions; and that, precisely with the removal of these conditions, those things that have arisen in dependence upon them-thus also all suffering-must perforce disappear and cease to be.]

SECOND STEP - RIGHT MINDEDNESS

WHAT, now, is Right Mindedness? It is thoughts free from lust; thoughts free from ill-will; thoughts free from cruelty. This is called right mindedness.

Now, Right Mindedness, let me tell you, is of two kinds: 1. Thoughts free from lust, from ill-will, and from cruelty:-this is called the "Mundane Right Mindedness," which yields worldly fruits and brings good results.

2. But, whatsoever there is of thinking, considering, reasoning, thought, ratiocination, application-the mind being holy, being turned away from the world, and conjoined with the path, the holy path being pursued-: these "Verbal Operations" of the mind are called the "Ultramundane Right Mindedness which is not of the world, but is ultra mundane, and conjoined with the paths.

Now, in understanding wrong-mindedness as wrong, and right-mindedness as right, one practices Right Understanding [1st step]; and in making efforts to overcome evil-mindedness, and to arouse right-mindedness, one practices Right Effort [6th step]; and in overcoming evil-mindedness with attentive mind, and dwelling with attentive mind in possession of right-mindedness, one practices Right Attentiveness [7th step]. Hence, there are three things that accompany and follow upon right-mindedness, namely: right understanding, right effort, and right attentiveness. THIRD STEP

THIRD STEP - RIGHT SPEECH

WHAT, now, is Right Speech? It is abstaining from lying; abstaining from tale-bearing; abstaining from harsh language; abstaining from vain talk.

There, someone avoids lying, and abstains from it. He speaks the truth, is devoted to the truth, reliable, worthy of confidence, is not a deceiver of men. Being at a meeting, or amongst people, or in the midst of his relatives, or in a society, or in the king's court, and called upon and asked as witness, to tell what he knows, he answers, if he knows nothing: "I know nothing"; and if he knows, he answers: "I know"; if he has seen nothing, he answers: "I have seen nothing," and if he has seen, he answers: "I have seen." Thus, he never knowingly speaks a lie, neither for the sake of his own advantage, nor for the sake of another person's advantage, nor for the sake of any advantage whatsoever.

He avoids tale-bearing, and abstains from it. What he has heard here, he does not repeat there, so as to cause dissension there; and what he heard there, he does not repeat here, so as to cause dissension here. Thus he unites those that are divided; and those that are united, he encourages. Concord gladdens him, he delights and rejoices in concord, and it is concord that he spreads by his words.

He avoids harsh language, and abstains from it. He speaks such words as are gentle, soothing to the ear, loving, going to the heart, courteous and dear, and agreeable to many.

[In Majjhima-Nikaya, No. 21, the Buddha says: "Even, O monks, should robbers and murderers saw through your limbs and joints, whoso gave way to anger thereat, would not be following my advice. For thus ought you to train yourselves:

"'Undisturbed shall our mind remain, no evil words shall escape our lips; friendly and full of sympathy shall we remain, with heart full of love, and free from any hidden malice; and that person shall we penetrate with loving thoughts, wide, deep, boundless, freed from anger and hatred.'"]

He avoids vain talk, and abstains from it. He speaks at the right time, in accordance with facts, speaks what is useful, speaks about the law and the discipline; his speech is like a treasure, at the right moment accompanied by arguments, moderate and full of sense.

This is called right speech.

Now, right speech, let me tell you, is of two kinds: 1. Abstaining from lying, from tale-bearing, from harsh language, and from vain talk; this is called the "Mundane Right Speech, which yields worldly fruits and brings good results.

2. But the abhorrence of the practice of this four-fold wrong speech, the abstaining, withholding, refraining therefrom-the mind being holy, being turned away from the world, and conjoined with the path, the holy path being pursued-: this is called the "Ultramundane Right Speech, which is not of the world, but is ultramundane, and conjoined with the paths.

Now, in understanding wrong speech as wrong, and right speech as right, one practices Right Understanding [1st step); and in making efforts to overcome evil speech and to arouse right speech, one practices Right Effort [6th step]; and in overcoming wrong speech with attentive mind, and dwelling with attentive mind in possession of right speech, one practices Right Attentiveness [7th step]. Hence, there are three things that accompany and follow upon right attentiveness.

FOURTH STEP - RIGHT ACTION

WHAT, now, is Right Action? It is abstaining from killing; abstaining from stealing; abstaining from unlawful sexual intercourse.

There, someone avoids the killing of living beings, and abstains from it. Without stick or sword, conscientious, full of sympathy, he is anxious for the welfare of all living beings.

He avoids stealing, and abstains from it; what another person possesses of goods and chattels in the village or in the wood, that he does not take away with thievish intent.

He avoids unlawful sexual intercourse, and abstains from it. He has no intercourse with such persons as are still under the protection of father, mother, brother, sister or relatives, nor with married women, nor female convicts, nor, lastly, with betrothed girls.

This is called Right Action.

Now, Right Action, let me tell you, is of two kinds: 1. Abstaining from killing, from stealing, and from unlawful sexual intercourse-this is called the "Mundane Right Action, which yields worldly fruits and brings good results. But the abhorrence of the practice of this three-fold wrong action, the abstaining, withholding, refraining therefrom-the mind being holy, being turned away from the world, and conjoined with the path, the holy path being pursued-: this is called the "Ultramundane Right Action," which is not of the world, but is ultramundane, and conjoined with the paths.

Now, in understanding wrong action as wrong, and right action as right, one practices Right Understanding [1st step]; and in making efforts to overcome wrong action, and to arouse right action, one practices Right Effort [6th step]; and in overcoming wrong action with attentive mind, and dwelling with attentive mind in possession of right action, one practices Right Attentiveness [7th step]. Hence, there are three things that accompany and follow upon right action, namely: right understanding, right effort, and right attentiveness.

FIFTH STEP - RIGHT LIVING

WHAT, now, is Right Living? When the noble disciple, avoiding a wrong way of living, gets his livelihood by a right way of living, this is called Right Living.

Now, right living, let me tell you, is of two kinds: 1. When the noble disciple, avoiding wrong living, gets his livelihood by a right way of living-this is called the "Mundane Right Living," which yields worldly fruits and brings good results.

2. But the abhorrence of wrong living, the abstaining, withholding, refraining therefrom-the mind being holy, being turned away from the world, and conjoined with the path, the holy path being pursued-: this is called the "Ultramundane Right Living," which is not of the world, but is ultramundane, and conjoined with the paths.

Now, in understanding wrong living as wrong, and right living as right, one practices Right Understanding [1st step]; and in making efforts to overcome wrong living, to arouse right living, one practices Right Effort [6th step]; and in overcoming wrong living with attentive mind, and dwelling with attentive mind in possession of right living, one practices Right Attentiveness [7th step]. Hence, there are three things that accompany and follow upon right living, namely: right understanding, right effort, and right attentiveness.

SIXTH STEP - RIGHT EFFORT

WHAT, now, is Right Effort? There are Four Great Efforts: the effort to avoid, the effort to overcome, the effort to develop, and the effort to maintain.

What, now, is the effort to avoid? There, the disciple incites his mind to avoid the arising of evil, demeritorious things that have not yet arisen; and he strives, puts forth his energy, strains his mind and struggles.

Thus, when he perceives a form with the eye, a sound with the ear, an odor with the nose, a taste with the tongue, a contact with the body, or an object with the mind, he neither adheres to the whole, nor to its parts. And he strives to ward off that through which evil and demeritorious things, greed and sorrow, would arise, if he remained with unguarded senses; and he watches over his senses, restrains his senses.

Possessed of this noble "Control over the Senses," he experiences inwardly a feeling of joy, into which no evil thing can enter. This is called the effort to avoid.

What, now, is the effort to Overcome? There, the disciple incites his mind to overcome the evil, demeritorious things that have already arisen; and he strives, puts forth his energy, strains his mind and struggles.

He does not retain any thought of sensual lust, ill-will, or grief, or any other evil and demeritorious states that may have arisen; he abandons them, dispels them, destroys them, causes them to disappear.

FIVE METHODS OF EXPELLING EVIL THOUGHTS

If, whilst regarding a certain object, there arise in the disciple, on account of it, evil and demeritorious thoughts connected with greed, anger and delusion, then the disciple should, by means of this object, gain another and wholesome object. Or, he should reflect on the misery of these thoughts: "Unwholesome, truly, are these thoughts! Blameable are these thoughts! Of painful result are these thoughts!" Or, he should pay no attention to these thoughts. Or, he should consider the compound nature of these thoughts. Or, with teeth clenched and tongue pressed against the gums, he should, with his mind, restrain, suppress and root out these thoughts; and in doing so, these evil and demeritorious thoughts of greed, anger and delusion will dissolve and disappear; and the mind will inwardly become settled and calm, composed and concentrated.

This is called the effort to overcome.

What, now, is the effort to Develop? There the disciple incites his will to arouse meritorious conditions that have not yet arisen; and he strives, puts forth his energy, strains his mind and struggles.

Thus he develops the "Elements of Enlightenment," bent on solitude, on detachment, on extinction, and ending in deliverance, namely: Attentiveness, Investigation of the Law, Energy, Rapture, Tranquility, Concentration, and Equanimity. This is called the effort to develop.

What, now, is the effort to Maintain? There, the disciple incites his will to maintain the meritorious conditions that have already arisen, and not to let them disappear, but to bring them to growth, to maturity and to the full perfection of development; and he strives, puts forth his energy, strains his mind and struggles.

Thus, for example, he keeps firmly in his mind a favorable object of concentration that has arisen, as the mental image of a skeleton, of a corpse infested by worms, of a corpse blue-black in color, of a festering corpse, of a corpse riddled with holes, of a corpse swollen up.

This is called the effort to maintain.

Truly, the disciple who is possessed of faith and has penetrated the Teaching of the Master, he is filled with the thought: "May rather skin, sinews and bones wither away, may the flesh and blood of my body dry up: I shall not give up my efforts so long as I have not attained whatever is attainable by manly perseverance, energy and endeavor!"

This is called right effort.

> The effort of Avoiding, Overcoming,
> Of Developing and Maintaining:
> These four great efforts have been shown
> By him, the scion of the sun.
> And he who firmly clings to them,
> May put an end to all the pain.

SEVENTH STEP -RIGHT ATTENTIVENESS

WHAT, now, is Right Attentiveness? The only way that leads to the attainment of purity, to the overcoming of sorrow and lamentation, to the end of pain and grief, to the entering upon the right path and the realization of Nirvana, is the "Four Fundamentals of Attentiveness." And which are these four? In them, the disciple dwells in contemplation of the Body, in contemplation of Feeling, in contemplation of the Mind, in contemplation of the Mind-objects, ardent, clearly conscious and attentive, after putting away worldly greed and grief.

CONTEMPLATION OF THE BODY

But, how does the disciple dwell in contemplation of the body? There, the disciple retires to the forest, to the foot of a tree, or to a solitary place, sits himself down, with legs crossed, body erect, and with attentiveness fixed before him.

With attentive mind he breathes in, with attentive mind he breathes out. When making a long inhalation, he knows: "I make a long inhalation"; when making a long exhalation, he knows: "I make a long exhalation." when making a short inhalation, he knows: "I make a short inhalation"; when making a short exhalation, he knows: "I make a short exhalation." "Clearly perceiving the entire [breath]-body, I will breathe in": thus he trains himself; "clearly perceiving the entire [breath]-body, I will breathe out": thus he trains himself. "Calming this bodily function, I will breathe n": thus he trains himself; "calming this bodily function, I will breathe out": thus he trains himself.

Thus he dwells in contemplation of the body, either with regard to his own person, or to other persons, or to both. He beholds how the body arises; beholds how it passes away; beholds the arising and passing away of the body. "A body is there-

"A body is there, but no living being, no individual, no woman,
no man, no self, and nothing that belongs to a self; neither a
person, nor anything belonging to a person"- this clear consciousness is present in him, because of his knowledge and mindfulness, and he lives independent, unattached to anything in the world. Thus does the disciple dwell in contemplation of the body.

And further, whilst going, standing, sitting, or lying down, the disciple understands the expressions: "I go"; "I stand"; "I sit"; "I lie down"; he understands any position of the body.

[The disciple understands that it is not a being, a real Ego, that goes, stands, etc., but that it is by a mere figure of speech that one says: "I go," "I stand," and so forth.]

And further, the disciple is clearly conscious in his going and coming; clearly conscious in looking forward and backward; clearly conscious in bending and stretching; clearly conscious in eating, drinking, chewing, and tasting; clearly conscious in discharging excrement and urine; clearly conscious in walking, standing, sitting, falling asleep and awakening; clearly conscious in speaking and in keeping silent.

"In all the disciple is doing, he is clearly conscious: of his intention, of his advantage, of his duty, of the reality."

And further, the disciple contemplates this body from the sole of the foot upward, and from the top of the hair downward, with a skin stretched over it, and filled with manifold impurities: "This body consists of hairs, nails, teeth, skin, flesh, sinews, bones, marrow, kidneys, heart, liver, diaphragm, spleen, lungs, intestines, bowels, stomach, and excrement; of bile, phlegm, pus, blood, sweat, lymph, tears, semen, spittle, nasal mucus, oil of the joints, and urine."

Just as if there were a sack, with openings at both ends, filled with all kinds of grain-with paddy, beans, sesamum and husked rice-and a man not blind opened it and examined its contents, thus: "That is paddy, these are beans, this is sesamum, this is husked rice": just so does the disciple investigate this body.

And further, the disciple contemplates this body with regard to the elements: "This body consists of the solid element, the liquid element, the heating element and the vibrating element." Just as a skilled butcher or butcher's apprentice, who has slaughtered a cow and divided it into separate portions, should sit down at the junction of four highroads: just so does the disciple contemplate this body with regard to the elements.

And further, just as if the disciple should see a corpse thrown into the burial-ground, one, two, or three days dead, swollen-up, blue-black in color, full of corruption he draws the conclusion as to his own body: "This my body also has this nature, has this destiny, and cannot escape it." And further, just as if the disciple should see a corpse thrown into the burial-ground, eaten by crows, hawks or vultures, by dogs or jackals, or gnawed by all kinds of worms-he draws the conclusion as to his own body: "This my body also has this nature, has this destiny, and cannot escape it."

And further, just as if the disciple should see a corpse thrown into the burial-ground, a framework of bones, flesh hanging from it, bespattered with blood, held together by the sinews; a framework of bones, stripped of flesh, bespattered with blood, held together by the sinews; a framework of bones, without flesh and blood, but still held together by the sinews; bones, disconnected and scattered in all directions, here a bone of the hand, there a bone of the foot, there a shin bone, there a thigh bone, there the pelvis, there the spine, there the skull-he draws the conclusion as to his own body: "This my body also has this nature, has this destiny, and cannot escape it."

And further, just as if the disciple should see bones lying in the burial ground, bleached and resembling shells; bones heaped together, after the lapse of years; bones weathered and crumbled to dust;-he draws the conclusion as to his own body: "This my body also has this nature, has this destiny, and cannot escape it "

Thus he dwells in contemplation of the body, either with regard to his own person, or to other persons, or to both. He beholds how the body arises; beholds how it passes away; beholds the arising and passing of the body. "A body is there" this clear consciousness is present in him, because of his knowledge and mindfulness; and he lives independent, unattached to anything in the world. Thus does the disciple dwell in contemplation of the body.

THE TEN BLESSINGS

Once the contemplation of the body is practiced, developed, often repeated, has become one's habit, one's foundation, is firmly established, strengthened and well perfected, one may expect ten blessings:

Over Delight and Discontent one has mastery; one does not allow himself to be overcome by discontent; one subdues it, as soon as it arises. One conquers Fear and Anxiety; one does not allow himself to be overcome by fear and anxiety; one subdues them, as soon as they arise. One endures cold and heat, hunger and thirst, wind and sun, attacks by gadflies, mosquitoes and reptiles; patiently one endures wicked and malicious speech, as well as bodily pains, that befall one, though they be piercing, sharp, bitter, unpleasant, disagreeable and dangerous to life. The four "Trances," the mind bestowing happiness even here: these one may enjoy at will, without difficulty, without effort.

One may enjoy the different "Magical Powers." With the "Heavenly Ear," the purified, the super-human, one may hear both kinds of sounds, the heavenly and the earthly, the distant and the near. With the mind one may obtain "Insight into the Hearts of Other Beings of other persons. One may obtain "Remembrance of many Previous Births." With the "Heavenly Eye," the purified, the super-human, one may see beings vanish and reappear, the base and the noble, the beautiful and the ugly, the happy and the unfortunate; one may perceive how beings are reborn according to their deeds.

One may, through the "Cessation of Passions," come to know for oneself, even in this life, the stainless deliverance of mind, the deliverance through wisdom.

CONTEMPLATION OF THE FEELINGS

But how does the disciple dwell in contemplation of the feelings?

In experiencing feelings, the disciple knows: "I have an indifferent agreeable feeling," or "I have a disagreeable feeling," or "I have an indifferent feeling," or "I have a worldly agreeable feeling," or "I have an unworldly agreeable feeling," or "I have a worldly disagreeable feeling," or "I have an unworldly disagreeable feeling," or "I have a worldly indifferent feeling," or have an unworldly indifferent feeling.

Thus he dwells in contemplation of the feelings, either with regard to his own person, or to other persons, or to both. He beholds how the feelings arise; beholds how they pass away; beholds the arising and passing away of the feelings. "Feelings are there": this clear consciousness is present in him, because of his knowledge and mindfulness; and he lives independent, unattached to anything in the world. Thus does the disciple dwell in contemplation of the feelings.

[The disciple understands that the expression "I feel" has no validity except as an expression of common speech; he understands that, in the absolute sense, there are only feelings, and that there is no Ego, no person, no experience of the feelings.]

CONTEMPLATION OF THE MIND

But how does the disciple dwell in contemplation of the mind? The disciple knows the greedy mind as greedy, and the not greedy mind as not greedy; knows the angry mind as angry, and the not angry mind as not angry; knows the deluded mind as deluded, and the undeluded mind as undeluded. He knows the cramped mind as cramped, and the scattered mind as scattered; knows the developed mind as developed, and the undeveloped mind as undeveloped; knows the surpassable mind as surpassable, and the unsurpassable mind as unsurpassable; knows the concentrated mind as concentrated, and the unconcentrated mind as unconcentrated; knows the freed mind as freed, and the unfreed mind as unfreed.

["Mind" is here used as a collective for the moments of consciousness. Being identical with consciousness, it should not be translated by "thought." "Thought" and "thinking" correspond rather to the so-called "verbal operations of the mind"; they are not, like consciousness, of primary, but of secondary nature, and are entirely absent in all sensuous consciousness, as well as in the second, third and fourth Trances. (See eighth step).]

Thus he dwells in contemplation of the mind, either with regard to his own person, or to other persons, or to both. He beholds how consciousness arises; beholds how it passes away; beholds the arising and passing away of consciousness. "Mind is there"; this clear consciousness is present in him, because of his knowledge and mindfulness; and he lives independent, unattached to anything in the world. Thus does the disciple dwell in contemplation of the mind.

CONTEMPLATION OF PHENOMENA (Mind-objects)

But how does the disciple dwell in contemplation of the phenomena? First, the disciple dwells in contemplation of the phenomen, of the "Five Hindrances."

He knows when there is "Lust" in him: "In me is lust"; knows when there is "Anger" in him: "In me is anger"; knows when there is "Torpor and Drowsiness" in him: "In me is torpor and drowsiness"; knows when there is "Restlessness and Mental Worry" in him: "In me is restlessness and mental worry"; knows when there are "Doubts" in him: "In me are doubts." He knows when these hindrances are not in him: "In me these hindrances are not." He knows how they come to arise; knows how, once arisen, they are overcome; knows how, once overcome, they do not rise again in the future.

[For example, Lust arises through unwise thinking on the agreeable and delightful. it may be suppressed by the following six methods: fixing the mind upon an idea that arouses disgust; contemplation of the loathsomeness of the body; controlling one's six senses; moderation in eating; friendship with wise and good men; right instruction. Lust is forever extinguished upon entrance into Anagamiship; Restlessness is extinguished by reaching Arahatship; Mental Worry, by reaching Sotapanship.]

And further: the disciple dwells in contemplation of the phenomena, of the five Groups of Existence. He knows what Corporeality is, how it arises, how it passes away; knows what Feeling is, how it arises, how it away; knows what Perception is, how it arises, how it passes away; knows what the Mental Formations are, how they arise, how they pass away; knows what Consciousness is, how it arises, how it passes away.

And further: the disciple dwells in contemplation of the phenomena of the six Subjective-Objective Sense-Bases. He knows eye and visual objects, ear and sounds, nose and odors, tongue and tastes, body and touches, mind and mind objects; and the fetter that arises in dependence on them, he also knows. He knows how the fetter comes to arise, knows how the fetter is overcome, and how the abandoned fetter does not rise again in future.

And further: the disciple dwells in contemplation of the phenomena of the seven Elements of Enlightenment. The disciple knows when there is Attentiveness in him; when there is Investigation of the Law in him; when there is Energy in him; when there is Enthusiasm in him; when there is Tranquility in him; when there is Concentration in him; when there is

Equanimity in him. He knows when it is not in him, knows how it comes to arise, and how it is fully developed.

And further: the disciple dwells in contemplation of the phenomena of the Four Noble Truths. He knows according to reality, what Suffering is; knows according to reality, what the Origin of Suffering is; knows according to reality, what the Extinction of Suffering is; knows according to reality, what the Path is that leads to the Extinction of Suffering.

Thus he dwells in contemplation of the phenomena, either with regard to his own person, or to other persons, or to both. He beholds how the phenomena arise; beholds how they pass away; beholds the arising and passing away of the phenomena. "Phenomena are there this consciousness is present in him because of his knowledge and mindfulness; and he lives independent, unattached to anything in the world. Thus does the disciple dwell in contemplation of the phenomena.

The only way that leads to the attainment of purity, to the overcoming of sorrow and lamentation, to the end of pain and grief, to the entering upon the right path, and the realization of Nirvana, is these four fundamentals of attentiveness.

NIRVANA THROUGH WATCHING OVER BREATHING

"Watching over In-and Out-breathing" practiced and developed, brings the four Fundamentals of Attentiveness to perfection; the four fundamentals of attentiveness, practiced and developed bring the seven Elements of Enlightenment to perfection; the seven elements of enlightenment, practiced and developed, bring Wisdom and Deliverance to perfection.

But how does Watching over In-and Out-breathing, practiced and developed, bring the four Fundamentals of Attentiveness to perfection?

I. Whenever the disciple is conscious in making a long inhalation or exhalation, or in making a short inhalation or exhalation, or is training himself to inhale or exhale whilst feeling the whole [breath]-body, or whilst calming down this bodily function-at such a time the disciple is dwelling in "contemplation of the body," of energy, clearly conscious, attentive, after subduing worldly greed and grief. For, inhalation and exhalation I call one amongst the corporeal phenomena.

II. Whenever the disciple is training himself to inhale or exhale whilst feeling rapture, or joy, or the mental functions, or whilst calming down the mental functions-at such a time he is dwelling in "contemplation of the feelings," full of energy, clearly conscious, attentive, after subduing worldly greed and grief. For, the full awareness of in-and outbreathing I call one amongst the feelings.

III. Whenever the disciple is training himself to inhale or exhale whilst feeling the mind, or whilst gladdening the mind or whilst concentrating the mind, or whilst setting the mind free-at such a time he is dwelling in "contemplation of the mind," full of energy, clearly conscious, attentive, after subduing worldly greed and grief. For, without attentiveness and clear consciousness, I say, there is no Watching over in-and Out-breathing.

IV. Whenever the disciple is training himself to inhale or exhale whilst contemplating impermanence, or the fading away of passion, or extinction, or detachment at such a time he is dwelling in "contemplation of the phenomena," full of energy, clearly conscious, attentive, after subduing worldly greed and grief.

Watching over In-and Out-breathing, thus practiced and developed, brings the four Fundamentals of Attentiveness to perfection.

But how do the four Fundamentals of Attentiveness, practiced and developed, bring the seven Elements of Enlightenment to full perfection?

Whenever the disciple is dwelling in contemplation of body, feeling, mind and phenomena, strenuous, clearly conscious, attentive, after subduing worldly greed and grief-at such a time his attentiveness is undisturbed; and whenever his attentiveness is present and undisturbed, at such a time he has gained and is developing the Element of Enlightenment "Attentiveness"; and thus this element of enlightenment reaches fullest perfection.

And whenever, whilst dwelling with attentive mind, he wisely investigates, examines and thinks over the Law-at such a time he has gained and is developing the Element of Enlightenment "Investigation of the Law"; and thus this element of enlightenment reaches fullest perfection.

And whenever, whilst wisely investigating, examining and thinking over the law, his energy is firm and unshaken-at such a time he has gained and is developing the Element of Enlightenment "Energy"; and thus this element of enlightenment reaches fullest perfection.

And whenever in him, whilst firm in energy, arises supersensuous rapture-at such a time he has gained and is developing the Element of Enlightenment "Rapture"; and thus this element of enlightenment reaches fullest perfection.

And whenever, whilst enraptured in mind, his spiritual frame and his mind become tranquil-at such a time he has gained and is developing the Element of Enlightenment "Tranquility"; and thus this element of enlightenment reaches fullest perfection.

And whenever, whilst being tranquilized in his spiritual frame and happy, his mind becomes concentrated-at such a time he has gained and is developing the Element of Enlightenment "Concentration; and thus this element of enlightenment reaches fullest perfection.

And whenever he thoroughly looks with indifference on his mind thus concentrated-at such a time he has gained and is developing the Element of Enlightenment "Equanimity."

The four fundamentals of attentiveness, thus practiced and developed, bring the seven elements of enlightenment to full perfection.

But how do the seven elements of enlightenment, practiced and developed, bring Wisdom and Deliverance to full perfection?

There, the disciple is developing the elements of enlightenment: Attentiveness, Investigation of the Law, Energy, Rapture, Tranquility, Concentration and Equanimity, bent on detachment, on absence of desire, on extinction and renunciation.

Thus practiced and developed, do the seven elements of enlightenment bring wisdom and deliverance to full perfection.

Just as the elephant hunter drives a huge stake into the ground and chains the wild elephant to it by the neck, in order to drive out of him his wonted forest ways and wishes, his forest unruliness, obstinacy and violence, and to accustom him to the environment of the village, and to teach him such good behavior as is required amongst men: in like manner also has the noble disciple to fix his mind firmly to these four fundamentals of attentiveness, so that he may drive out of himself his wonted worldly ways and wishes, his wonted worldly unruliness, obstinacy and violence, and win to the True, and realize Nirvana.

EIGHTH STEP - RIGHT CONCENTRATION

WHAT, now, is Right Concentration? Fixing the mind to a single object ("One-pointedness of mind"): this is concentration.

The four Fundamentals of Attentiveness (seventh step): these are the objects of concentration.

The four Great Efforts (sixth step): these are the requisites for concentration.

The practicing, developing and cultivating of these things: this is the "Development" of concentration.

[Right Concentration has two degrees of development: 1. "Neighborhood-Concentration," which approaches the first trance, without however attaining it; 2. "Attainment Concentration," which is the concentration present in the four trances. The attainment of the trances, however, is not a requisite for the realization of the Four Ultramundane Paths of Holiness; and neither Neighborhood-Concentration nor Attainment-Concentration, as such, in any way possesses the power of conferring entry into the Four Ultramundane Paths; hence, in them is really no power to free oneself permanently from evil things. The realization of the Four Ultramundane Paths is possible only at the moment of insight into the impermanency, miserable nature, and impersonality of phenomenal process of existence. This insight is attainable only during Neighborhood-Concentration, not during Attainment-Concentration.

He who has realized one or other of the Four Ultramundane Paths without ever having attained the Trances, is called a "Dry-visioned One," or one whose passions are "dried up by Insight." He, however, who after cultivating the Trances has reached one of the Ultramundane Paths, is called "one who has taken tranquility as his vehicle."]

THE FOUR TRANCES

Detached from sensual objects, detached from unwholesome things, the disciple enters into the first trance, which is accompanied by "Verbal Though," and "Rumination," is born of "Detachment," and filled with "Rapture," and "Happiness."

This first trance is free from five things, and five things are present. When the disciple enters the first trance, there have vanished [the 5 Hindrances]: Lust, Ill-will, Torpor and Dullness, Restlessness and Mental Worry, Doubts; and there are present: Verbal Thought, Rumination, Rapture, Happiness, and Concentration.

And further: after the subsiding of verbal thought and rumination, and by the gaining of inward tranquility and oneness of mind, he enters into a state free from verbal thought and rumination, the second trance, which is born of Concentration, and filled with Rapture and Happiness.

And further: after the fading away of rapture, he dwells in equanimity, attentive, clearly conscious; and he experiences in his person that feeling, of which the Noble Ones say: "Happy lives the man of equanimity and attentive mind"-thus he enters the third trance.

And further: after the giving up of pleasure and pain, and through the disappearance of previous joy and grief, he enters into a state beyond pleasure and pain, into the fourth trance, which is purified by equanimity and attentiveness.

[The four Trances may be obtained by means of Watching over In-and Out-breathing, as well as through the fourth sublime meditation, the "Meditation of Equanimity," and others.

The three other Sublime Meditations of "Loving Kindness," "Compassion", and "Sympathetic Joy" may lead to the attainment of the first three Trances. The "Cemetery Meditations," as well as the meditation "On Loathsomeness," will produce only the First Trance.

The "Analysis of the Body," and the Contemplation on the Buddha, the Law, the Holy Brotherhood, Morality, etc., will only produce Neighborhood-Concentration.]

Develop your concentration: for he who has concentration understands things according to their reality. And what are these things? The arising and passing away of corporeality, of feeling, perception, mental formations and consciousness.

Thus, these five Groups of Existence must be wisely penetrated; Delusion and Craving must be wisely abandoned; Tranquility and Insight must be wisely developed.

This is the Middle Path which the Perfect One has discovered, which makes one both to see and to know, and which leads to peace, to discernment, to enlightenment, to Nirvana.

And following upon this path, you will put an end to suffering.

DEVELOPMENT OF THE EIGHTFOLD PATH IN THE DISCIPLE

CONFIDENCE AND RIGHT-MINDEDNESS (2nd Step)

SUPPOSE a householder, or his son, or someone reborn in any family, hears the law; and after hearing the law he is filled with confidence in the Perfect One. And filled with this confidence, he thinks: "Full of hindrances is household life, a refuse heap; but pilgrim life is like the open air. Not easy is it, when one lives at home, to fulfill in all points the rules of the holy life. How, if now I were to cut off hair and beard, put on the yellow robe and go forth from home to the homeless life?" And in a short time, having given up his more or less extensive possessions, having forsaken a smaller or larger circle of relations, he cuts off hair and beard, puts on the yellow robe, and goes forth from home to the homeless life.

MORALITY (3rd, 4th, 5th Step)

Having thus left the world, he fulfills the rules of the monks. He avoids the killing of living beings and abstains from it. Without stick or sword, conscientious, full of sympathy, he is anxious for the welfare of all living beings.-He avoids stealing, and abstains from taking what is not given to him. Only what is given to him he takes, waiting till it is given; and he lives with a heart honest and pure.-He avoids unchastity, living chaste, resigned, and keeping aloof from sexual intercourse, the vulgar way.-He avoids lying and abstains from it. He speaks the truth, is devoted to the truth, reliable, worthy of confidence, is not a deceiver of men.-He avoids tale-bearing and abstains from it. What he has heard here, he does not repeat there, so as to cause dissension there; and what he has heard there, he does not repeat here, so as to cause dissension here. Thus he unites those that are divided, and those that are united he encourages; concord gladdens him, he delights and rejoices in concord, and it is concord that he spreads by his words.-He avoids harsh language and abstains from it. He speaks such words as are gentle, soothing to the ear, loving, going to the heart, courteous and dear, and agreeable to many.- He avoids vain talk and abstains from it. He speaks at the right time, in accordance with facts, speaks what is useful, speaks about the law and the disciple; his speech is like a treasure, at the right moment accompanied by arguments, moderate, and full of sense.

He keeps aloof from dance, song, music and the visiting of shows; rejects flowers, perfumes, ointments, as well as every kind of adornment and embellishment. High and gorgeous beds he does not use. Gold and silver he does not accept. Raw corn and meat he does not accept. Women and girls he does not accept. He owns no male and female slaves, owns no goats, sheep, fowls, pigs, elephants, cows or horses, no land and goods. He does not go on errands and do the duties of a messenger. He keeps aloof from buying and selling things. He has nothing to do with false measures, metals and weights. He avoids the crooked ways of bribery, deception and fraud. He keeps aloof from stabbing, beating, chaining, attacking, plundering and oppressing.

He contents himself with the robe that protects his body, and with the alms with which he keeps himself alive. Wherever he goes, he is provided with these two things; just as a winged bird, in flying, carries his wings along with him. By fulfilling this noble Domain of Morality he feels in his heart an irreproachable happiness.

CONTROL OF THE SENSES (6th Step)

Now, in perceiving a form with the eye- a sound with the ear- an odor with the nose- a taste with the tongue- a touch with the body- an object with his mind, he sticks neither to the whole, nor to its details. And he tries to ward off that which, by being unguarded in his senses, might give rise to evil and unwholesome states, to greed and sorrow; he watches over his senses, keep his senses under control. By practicing this noble "Control of the Senses" he feels in his heart an unblemished happiness.

ATTENTIVENESS AND CLEAR CONSCIOUSNESS (7th Step)

Clearly conscious is he in his going and coming; clearly conscious in looking forward and backward; clearly conscious in bending and stretching his body; clearly conscious in eating, drinking, chewing and tasting; dearly conscious in discharging excrement and urine; clearly conscious in walking, standing, sitting, falling asleep and awakening; clearly conscious in speaking and keeping silent.

Now, being equipped with this lofty Morality, equipped with this noble Control of the Senses, and filled with this noble "Attentiveness and Clear Consciousness, he chooses a secluded dwelling in the forest, at the foot of a tree, on a mountain, in a cleft, in a rock cave, on a burial ground, on a woody table-land, in the open air, or on a heap of straw. Having returned from his alms-round, after the meal, he sits himself down with legs crossed, body erect, with attentiveness fixed before him.

ABSENCE OF THE FIVE HINDRANCES

He has cast away Lust; he dwells with a heart free from lust; from lust he cleanses his heart.

He has cast away Ill-will; he dwells with a heart free from ill-will; cherishing love and compassion toward all living beings, he cleanses his heart from ill-will.

He has cast away Torpor and Dullness; he dwells free from torpor and dullness; loving the light, with watchful mind, with clear consciousness, he cleanses his mind from torpor and dullness.

He has cast away Restlessness and Mental Worry; dwelling with mind undisturbed, with heart full of peace, he cleanses his mind from restlessness and mental worry.

He has cast away Doubt; dwelling free from doubt, full of confidence in the good, he cleanses his heart from doubt.

THE TRANCES (8th Step)

He has put aside these five Hindrances and come to know the paralyzing corruptions of the mind. And far from sensual impressions, far from unwholesome things, he enters into the Four Trances.

INSIGHT (1st Step)

But whatsoever there is of feeling, perception, mental formation, or consciousness-all these phenomena he regards as "impermanent," "subject to pain," as infirm, as an ulcer, a thorn, a misery, a burden, an enemy, a disturbance, as empty and "void of an Ego"; and turning away from these things, he directs his mind towards the abiding, thus: "This, verily, is the Peace, this is the Highest, namely the end of all formations, the forsaking of every substratum of rebirth, the fading away of craving; detachment, extinction: Nirvana." And in this state he reaches the "Cessation of Passions."

NIRVANA

And his heart becomes free from sensual passion, free from the passion for existence, free from the passion of ignorance. "Freed am I!": this knowledge arises in the liberated one; and he knows: "Exhausted is rebirth, fulfilled the Holy Life; what was to be done, has been done; naught remains more for this world to do."

Forever am I liberated,

This is the last time that I'm born,
No new existence waits for me.

This, verily, is the highest, holiest wisdom: to know that all suffering has passed away.

This, verily, is the highest, holiest peace: appeasement of greed, hatred and delusion.

THE SILENT THINKER

"I am" is a vain thought; "I am not" a vain thought; "I shall be" is a vain thought; "I shall not be" is a vain thought. Vain thoughts are a sickness, an ulcer, a thorn. But after overcoming all vain thoughts, one is called silent thinker." And the thinker, the Silent One, does no more arise, no more pass away, no more tremble, no more desire. For there is nothing in him that he should arise again. And as he arises no more, how should he grow old again? And as he grows no more old, how should he die again? And as he dies no more, how should he tremble? And as he trembles no more, how should he have desire?

THE TRUE GOAL

Hence, the purpose of the Holy Life does not consist in acquiring alms, honor, or fame, nor in gaining morality, concentration, or the eye of knowledge. That unshakable deliverance of the heart: that, verily, is the object of the Holy Life, that is its essence, that is its goal.

And those, who formerly, in the past, were Holy and Enlightened Ones, those Blessed Ones also have pointed out to their disciples this self-same goal, as has been pointed out by me to my disciples. And those, who afterwards, in the future, will be Holy and Enlightened Ones, those Blessed Ones also will point out to their disciples this self-same goal, as has been pointed out by me to my disciples.

However, Disciples, it may be that (after my passing away) you might think: "Gone is the doctrine of our Master. We have no Master more." But you should not think; for the Law and the Discipline, which I have taught you, Will, after my death, be your master.

The Law be your light,
The Law be your refuge!
Do not look for any other refuge!

Disciples, the doctrines, which I advised you to penetrate, you should well preserve, well guard, so that this Holy Life may take its course and continue for ages, for the weal and welfare of the many, as a consolation to the world, for the happiness, weal and welfare of heavenly beings and men.

27232354R00031

Printed in Great Britain
by Amazon